This book belongs to

_____

Barack Obama

By Mary Nhin

Illustrated By
Yuliia Zolotova

This book is dedicated to my children - Mikey, Kobe, and Jojo.

Copyright © 2022 by Grow Grit Press LLC. All rights reserved. No part of this book may be reproduced in any form without permission in writing from the publisher. Please send bulk order requests to growgritpress@gmail.com 978-1-63731-353-4 Printed and bound in the USA. MiniMovers.tv

Hi, I'm
Barack Obama.

I was born in Hawaii to an interracial couple. My mom was an American woman with European heritage and my father was a black man from Kenya.

My parents divorced when I was three years old
and my father moved away. For a time, I lived with
my mother in Indonesia, but I eventually came back
to Hawaii to live with my grandmother.

I went to a private school where I was one of only a few students who were black. This could have been a very lonely experience, but the culture there was respectful and there were students of many different cultural heritages. The cultural diversity allowed me to gain a great variety of experiences and to become very proud of my mixed-race heritage.

It also taught me to see and listen to the experiences of others and gave me a strong belief in equality. This core value drove me to dedicate my life's work to standing up for all people.

Only 1.2% of the student body was black, so I did experience some racial tensions. I struggled those years to understand my multicultural heritage.

The future rewards those who press on. I don't have time to feel sorry for myself. I don't have time to complain. I'm going to press on.

I worked hard at school and was offered a full scholarship to Northwestern University School of Law. But I really wanted to go to Harvard Law School, so that's where I enrolled.

I was elected the first black president of the Harvard Law Review. This led to my first book deal in which I wrote Dreams From My Father.

Soon after, I accepted a position to teach at the University of Chicago Law School. During this time, I enjoyed supporting disadvantaged communities by ensuring that people knew they could have their say by using their vote.

My next adventure was working as a lawyer to stand up for people's civil rights. I felt hopeful I could make a difference and this soon led me to become a politician.

In 1996, I ran for office and was successfully elected State Senator of Illinois. It was a great accomplishment and I was very happy! But I wasn't done. I soon announced I would be running for president.

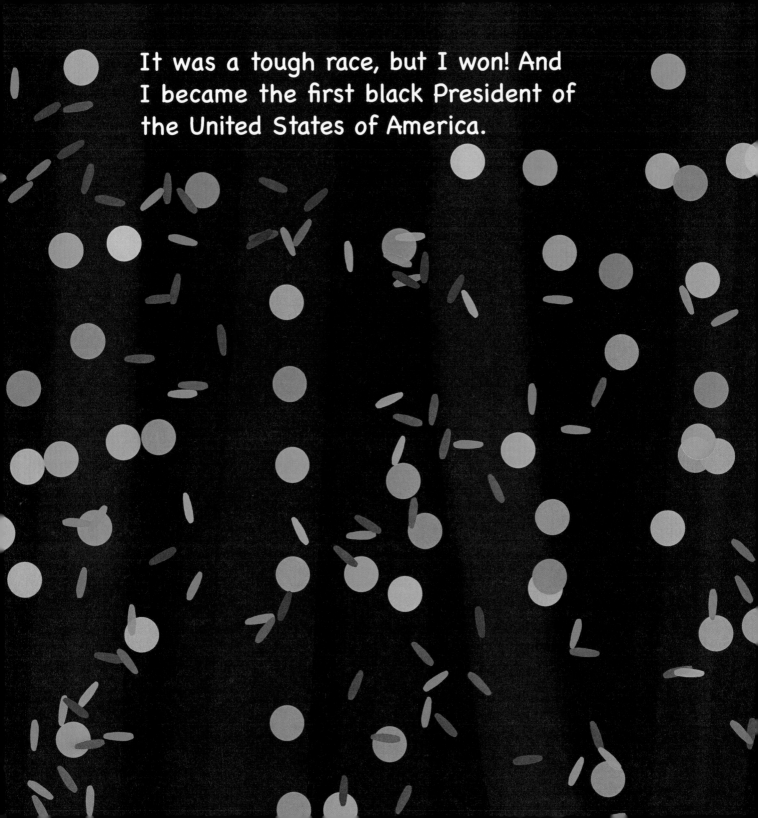

It was a tough race, but I won! And I became the first black President of the United States of America.

I hope that the next generation of world leaders will continue to support people from all different backgrounds like I have. And I hope that I have inspired people around the world to be kind and stand up for each other, no matter what our differences may be.

Timeline

1991 – Barack graduates magna cum laude from
       Harvard Law School

1992 – Barack marries Michelle Robinson

1996 – Barack becomes U.S. Senator

2005 – Barack is awarded the NAACP Chairman's Award

2008 – Barack wins U.S. Presidential election

2009 – Barack wins the Nobel Peace Prize

2013 – Barack begins second term as President
       of the U.S.

2017 – Barack receives the John. F. Kennedy
       Profile in Courage Award

minimovers.tv

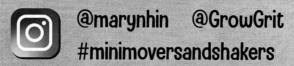 @marynhin   @GrowGrit
#minimoversandshakers

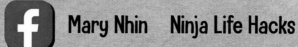 Mary Nhin   Ninja Life Hacks

Ninja Life Hacks

 @ninjalifehacks.tv

Made in United States
North Haven, CT
05 September 2023

41195818R00022